Jack and the Be

About the book

When there is no food in the cupboard, Jack goes to market to sell Daisy the cow. But rather than money, Jack swaps Daisy for some magic beans and the promise of adventure. This results in a fit of rage from his mother, who throws the beans out of the window and into the garden. However, as in all good fairy tales, magic comes to the rescue and the beanstalk mysteriously weaves its way into the story. In a dreamlike state, Jack fearlessly enters the world of the giant. He watches from afar and soon makes plans to liberate the giant's treasures.

This retelling can be seen as a magical tale about how faith and belief in something will get you far and about how optimism will help you when things are tough. Yet it also stimulates thought-provoking questions, such as is wealth a good thing? Can stealing ever be justified? Do we deserve wealth if we have not worked for it?

The book provides children with opportunities to become storytellers within the familiar framework of this well-known traditional tale. It is an exciting stimulus for discussion about things that are important to us and offers opportunities for scientific and geographical enquiry. The wonderful illustrations are dreamlike and quirky and help young readers to engage with Jack's sense of playful exploration. Children will be inspired to create their own magic lands where the impossible may become possible. There are many opportunities for creativity in a variety of media, such as dance, drama, art and music. Like all good tales, *Jack and the Beanstalk* will be remembered for a lifetime and passed down to future generations.

About the author

The late Richard Walker was a published author and editor of books for children and young adults. He was a professional storyteller who told his tales in venues around the UK. He also edited *Facts & Fiction,* the storytelling magazine. He wrote his first book for children, *The Barefoot Book of Trickster Tales,* in 1998. This was followed by *The Barefoot Book of Pirates.*

About the illustrator

Award-winning author and illustrator of children's books Niamh Sharkey grew up in Ireland. As a child she loved books and her best friend instilled in her a love of drawing, although she had several jobs including a waitress, a saleswoman and a lifeguard before deciding to draw for a living. In 1999, she won The Bisto Book of the Year Award for *Tales of Wisdom and Wonder.* In the same year she won The Mother Goose Award for *The Gigantic Turnip.* She has also written and illustrated her own children's stories including *The Ravenous Beast, Santasaurus* and *I'm a Happy Hugglewug.*

> **Facts and figures**
> It is suggested that the origins of the story of *Jack and the Beanstalk* grew out of the oral tradition in the 1700s. The story was also known as 'Jack the Giant Killer'.
> This retelling of *Jack and the Beanstalk* was first published in 1999 and was a finalist in *ForeWord Magazine's* Book of the Year Award in 2000.

Guided reading

Cover and title page

Display the cover of the book and invite the children to describe what they see.

Look at the illustration. Ask the children: *What sort of character does the illustration portray Jack as?* Challenge them to describe his outfit. What do they notice about his clothes? (The curls on his hat and shoes mimic the tendrils of the beanstalk plant.) Look together at the title. What do they notice about the font in terms of size and layout? (The text is undulating and the word *Jack* rises.) Could this represent the beanstalk?

Turn to the title page. Point out how the text is the same as the front cover. Look together at the illustrations. Can the children describe any similarities between the figures? Ask: *Which character appears to be slightly different?* (The old lady from the castle has pointed features rather than curled ones.) Challenge the children to guess who the characters are from their knowledge of the traditional tale. Explain that this story also contains a storyteller or narrator and ask them to identify him.

Point out that the author title uses the word *retold* because this is a retelling and not an original story. Ask the children if they are familiar with any other versions of this story and discuss whether these versions differ.

A little bit of this

Look at both blocks of text on the first page. Ask: *What is different about them?* (One half of the page is written in italics, the other in a bold font.) Read the first text block. Point out that it is written in the first person. Who do the children think the *I* refers to? Ask the children to define the role of a narrator or storyteller.

Read the phrase *a little bit of this and a little bit of that*. What might this mean? Can the children think of any phrases that might mean a similar thing? (For example, 'bits and bobs', 'odds and ends'.) Look carefully at the illustration on the opposite page. Ask: *What extra information does the illustration provide? Do the characters look*

lazy? What are they doing? What would you expect a lazy person to be like?

Read the second block of text together and point out that it is written in the third person. Ask the children which version is most familiar to them in the books they read.

The funny little man

Turn to the third double-page spread and cover the text on the right-hand page. Look together at the illustrations. Can the children predict what the text might say? Turn over and ask the children to tell you in their own words what happens next in the story. Read the text together and ask the children to recall the description of the little man. Now invite the children to offer their own descriptions of the man. What is the first thing they notice about him? Find the text that indicates that the man is speaking. Ask the children to suggest ways that he may speak. Ask: *Will he have a silly voice to match his appearance?*

Six magic beans

Turn to the next double-page spread and read the text together. Point out that the main focus of this page is on the beans. Ask the children to recall the three ways that the beans are described (*plump*, *ordinary* and *magic*). Ask the children to find additional words to describe the magic beans. Read the last paragraph of text again. Ask the children to think about the phrase *there was nothing Jack loved better than magic*. What would the children choose as the thing they loved nothing better than?

Describing characters

Read the text on the fifth double-page spread and ask the children to identify as many pieces of descriptive language as they can. Make a list of the things that describe Jack's actions and feelings. Do the same for Jack's mum. Challenge the children to use just one word to describe each of the characters.

Guided reading

The beans begin to grow

After reading the text on the following spread, cover up the words and ask the children to recall in sequence what happened when the beans landed in the garden. Can they remember any of the exact phrases? Look at the illustration. Ask: *What do you think the bugs might be thinking as they watch the beans grow?*

Exploring feelings

Before reading the text on the next spread, ask the children to think about the atmosphere created by the illustration. Ask them to help you to make a list of all the things that create this feeling. After reading the text, ask the children if they think Jack was scared. Point out that Jack asks only two questions. Ask: *What questions would you ask if this happened to you? Would you have climbed the beanstalk? Why/why not?*

Up above the clouds

Look first at the illustration on spread 8. What does the use of colour, the fluffy clouds and the mobile on top of the castle suggest? (A dreamlike scenario.) Read the text together and ask the children to recall what noises Jack heard and what made these noises. Can the children think of other things that might clank, rumble, rattle or creak?

Turn the page and read the text. Ask: *Which words did the little old woman whisper?* The words *GO AWAY!* are in large text. What does this indicate? Ask the children to whisper loudly.

The giant's coming!

Look at the text together on spread 10. Point out the word *he*. Show how the use of italics affects the sentence, reading it both with and without the emphasis. Continue reading the text. Think together about the use of descriptive language. Ask: *Which words describe the sacks? Which words describe the giant's footsteps?* Before turning the page, challenge the children to describe what they imagine the giant might look like.

Fee, Fi, Fo, Fum!

Look at the illustration of the giant on the next page; does he match any of the children's descriptions? Now look together at the text. What do the children notice first? (The text in the first line is enlarged.) Read the giant's rhyme to the children and ask if they have heard any other versions of it. Ask the children to join in the traditional rhyme using their giant voices.

Ask the children to identify more examples of the giant's speech and encourage them to read their examples in their giant voice. What do they notice about the giant's manners?

The harp and the goose

Read the text together on spread 12. Ask the children to discuss whether they would prefer the harp or the goose and why. Where do they think these things might have come from? Ask: *Do you like being in the giant's castle?*

Turn the page and cover the text. Ask the children to use story language to describe what is happening. Challenge them to use words to describe the noises Jack might hear as he steals the gold. Now read the text. Did the children's language bear any resemblance to the text?

Comic book sequence

Look at the layout of the next spread (it has a comic book appearance). Which order should you read the text in? Ask the children to describe the sequence of events on this spread. Think about the sequence and how this could be illustrated.

Turn over and look at the picture on the right-hand page of the next spread. Ask the children to predict what the goose and Jack might be saying to each other. Invite the children to help you create a thought bubble and a speech bubble for the old woman on the left-hand page to show what she might be thinking and saying.

Guided reading

He's behind you!

Read the text on the next spread to the children, creating as much dramatic effect as possible. Leave a pause after the final sentence on the left-hand page. Continue reading and when you have finished, ask the children to describe how they felt as you read the text. Which words helped to create the impression of a chase and the urgency of the escape? Point out that the last sentence is described as a cliffhanger. It is designed to leave the reader wondering what might happen next. Think together about some possible different endings.

Picture power

Turn the page and look together at the illustration. There is a sense of movement. Ask the children to think about words that might describe these movements. Now read the text, pointing out examples of movement words. Ask the children to predict what happens next. Can they think of any other traditional tales where things are pulled and pulled? ('The Enormous Turnip'.) Ask: *What happens when you stop pulling?* Look at the giant in the picture. How do the children think he is feeling at this moment?

Boing!

Ask the children to help you read out the long word written across the last spread. What noise do you think the giant might be making? Invite the children to try writing their own long sound-effect words. Read the text and ask the children to identify the sentence that reminds them that this has been a story told by a storyteller (*And, as far as I know…*). Turn to the final page and describe what is happening in each picture. Ask the children to tell their own happy endings in the first person as the storyteller.

Shared reading

Extract 1

- Read an enlarged copy of the text together.
- Look at the first sentence. Ask the children to identify two words that sound similar and circle them (*knew* and *argue*). Look carefully at the way the words are constructed. Which digraphs make the same sound in each word? Ask the children to sort the following words into the 'ew' or 'ue' category: blue, threw, glue, brew, stew, due.
- Draw a large picture of the funny little man with two big pockets. Ask the children to help you write 'funny little man' as a heading.
- Now ask them to help you sound out a label saying 'baggy jacket pocket'. Point out the common sounds of the two labels, for example, the end 'y' sound and the 'ck' sound.
- Give each child a small piece of paper and explain that they are going to fill the pockets of the funny little man with pictures of things that contain either of those sounds (rocket, bucket, bunny, honey…).

Extract 2

- Look together at the enlarged text and ask the children to suggest voices for the characters as each one speaks.
- Look closely at the first sentence together. Challenge the children to circle as many digraphs as they can. (They should find as many as 17.)
- Point out that two words contain 'oo' but that one makes the 'or' sound. Which digraph is repeated most in the sentence? Count how many different ones are not repeated. (There are 10.)
- Now look through the remaining text to find words that have apostrophes in them. (*What's, They're, we've, they've.*) Ask the children to say why these words need an apostrophe. (They are abbreviated words.) Which words have been shortened? (What is, they are, we have, they have.)
- Now look at the apostrophe in the word *Jack's*. Is this the same sort of apostrophe? Explain to the children that this is a possessive apostrophe and ask them to think of other examples of words that might fit into either category.

Extract 3

- Read the enlarged text together and ask the children to help you draw two rows of sacks, as shown in the illustration.
- Write the word 'giant' on one sack on the top row and the word 'got' on the first sack on the lower row. Ask the children to decode both words. What do they notice about the sound the letter makes in each case.
- Look back through the text again, stopping on any words that have a 'j' sound in them. If the word has a soft 'g' they should record that word on the top row of sacks (*huge, bulging, managed*). If they find a hard 'g' sound they must record it on the lower shelf of sacks (*big*). If it is a 'j' then it cannot be written on any of the sacks.
- Challenge the group to think of more words to fill all of the sacks on both shelves.

Extract 1

Jack knew better than to argue. Besides, he was very hungry. So the next day he got up at sunrise and set off down the lane with Daisy in tow.

He had not gone far when he came around a corner and bumped into a funny little man. The man was wearing a big, baggy jacket with big, baggy pockets.

'Good morning to you!' said the man. 'That's a nice-looking cow you have there. Do you fancy doing a swap for her?'

Text © 1999, Richard Walker; Illustrations © 1999, Niamh Sharkey.

Extract 2

As soon as he reached the back door, Jack burst into the kitchen and proudly threw the beans down on the table.

'What's this?' exclaimed his mum.

'Oh dear,' thought Jack.

'They're magic beans, Mum. I swapped them for Daisy. At least we've got something to eat… well, we will have when they've grown.'

Jack's mum was furious. She went white in the face and shouted and stamped.

Then she threw open the window and flung the beans outside.

That night, Jack and his mum went to bed feeling miserable and hungry.

Extract 3

'Who's *he*?' asked Jack as they made their way along the dusty castle corridors to the big kitchen. Lining the walls were mounds of huge, bulging sacks, which jingled as Jack brushed against them.

'The giant, of course. If he catches you, he'll eat you for sure. He's got a foul temper so you'd better keep out of his way. Hide among the sacks if you hear him coming.'

Then, just as she finished speaking, there was a crashing of heavy footsteps outside the room. Jack only just managed to hide behind a heap of sacks when the door burst open and in barged the giant.

Plot, character and setting

Noisy giant

Objective: To interpret a text by reading aloud with some variety in pace and emphasis.
What you need: Copies of *Jack and the Beanstalk*; an enlarged photocopiable page 15, a range of percussion instruments that can be banged or rattled such as claves, drumsticks, castanets, chime bars, xylophones, bells and shakers.
Cross-curricular link: Music.

What to do

● Look together at the pictures on the enlarged photocopiable page 15 which represent noisy parts of the story.
● Look through the book to identify and talk about where each noisy incident occurs and why.
● Look at the selection of instruments and ask the children to match one or more instruments to each illustration on the photocopiable sheet.

● Arrange the group into two. Ask one group to use the instruments while the other group reads the words to describe what is happening in the picture. Allow the groups to swap roles.
● Now read the words at the bottom of the photocopiable sheet and ask each child to choose an instrument that they can use to beat out the rhythm of the giant's chorus. Highlight and illustrate the word which has more than one syllable, stin/ky. Ask the children to tap out the rhythm as you all chant the words together.

Differentiation
For older/more confident learners: Ask children to extend the rhyme using words with more syllables.
For younger/less confident learners: Start the activity by tapping out children's names to familiarise them with one- and two-syllable words.

The giant and the harp dance

Objective: To explore familiar themes and characters through music, improvisation and role play.
What you need: Copies of *Jack and the Beanstalk*, 'Venus' and 'Mars' (from Holst's *The Planets Suite*), playback equipment, hall space, a flipchart and a pen.
Cross-curricular link: Dance.

What to do

● Play 'Venus' to the children and ask them to describe how the music makes them feel. Encourage them to use words or phrases that capture the sleepy atmosphere.
● Now play 'Mars' and, again, ask for a description of how the music makes them feel or what it reminds them of.
● Play the pieces of music again while the children look through their copy of the book. Ask the children to compare the two pieces of music.

Discuss pace and tone. Which instruments can be identified? Did the pieces evoke different moods, emotions, pictures? If so, what and why?
● Together, find places in the book that could be matched to the music. Prompt the children to think carefully about the giant's movements when awake and crashing about and when the harp plays to him.
● Record descriptive action words such as banging, stamping, crashing, nodding, yawning. Encourage the children to demonstrate examples of movements they could match to the music.

Differentiation
For older/more confident learners: Give children time to put their movements into a sequence and perform their dance with gesture and facial expression.
For younger/less confident learners: Model a variety of movements and actions for children to copy.

Plot, character and setting

Swap

> **Objective:** To visualise and comment on events, characters and ideas.
> **What you need:** Photocopiable page 16, scissors, pens.

What to do

● Give each child photocopiable page 16. Explain that, on the sheet, they will find four pictures of things that the giant treasures.

● Point out that there are also four blank spaces and invite the children to fill these in with pictures of things that they value greatly.

● When the children have completed their drawings, ask them to cut out all eight cards.

● Organise the children into pairs. Each pair should put all their cards together without sharing what they are and shuffle them.

● Tell the pairs to place one card in the middle and deal out the rest. The child with the most cards starts by turning over a card from their pile. If they think that the card in the middle is of a higher value to them, they can swap it by adding this card to their own pile and placing their unwanted card in the middle. Then allow the second child to take a turn.

● If two cards showing the same thing are revealed, the first person to say 'Snap' wins those cards. The game continues until one player runs out of cards.

> **Differentiation**
> **For older/more confident learners:** Encourage children to write labels for each card.
> **For younger/less confident learners:** Provide adult support or demonstrate how to play the game in a small group first.

Scavenger hunt

> **Objective:** To retell stories, ordering events using story language.
> **What you need:** Copies of *Jack and the Beanstalk*, access to outdoor space, four sets of laminated cards cut out from enlarged photocopiable page 17 and hidden randomly in locations around the outdoor space, large pieces of paper, gluesticks.

What to do

● Arrange the class into teams of four. Ask the children to think about the different objects that they might see in the story of Jack and the Beanstalk. Ask: *Which of these things are living things? Which are inanimate objects? Which could be described as magical?*

● Tell the children that hidden around the outside space are four sets of eight cards (one for each group). Explain that each set of eight cards depicts objects from the book.

● Challenge the groups to search for their set of cards and to put them in the order in which they appear in the book. For example, a cow would appear before a castle.

● As they find a card, ask the groups to bring it back to their base and stick it on their large piece of paper in the correct order.

● When all eight cards have been found and have been verified by the group as being in the correct order, the winner can be announced.

> **Differentiation**
> **For older/more confident learners:** Encourage children to add text under each card once it has been stuck on to the paper.
> **For younger/less confident learners:** Number some of the cards to help children order the sequence more easily.

Plot, character and setting

Magic beans

Objective: To explore familiar themes and characters through improvisation and role play.
What you need: Copies of *Jack and the Beanstalk*, a handful of dried runner beans, broad beans or similar to put in a velvet pouch or a special box.
Cross-curricular link: Drama.

What to do

● Look at the page where the beans are beginning to grow in the ground. Ask the children: *What do you think is happening to the beans?* (Maybe the magic is starting.)
● Explain that you have some magic beans in a special pouch (or box). Show it to the children and tell them that the beans inside can make people's voices do strange things. Explain that when they hold a bean it will make their voice change.

● Ask the children to tell you what voice each of the characters or objects in the book might have. For example, the harp might sing, the mother might be stern.
● What would the goose sound like? Explore ideas for the funny little man, the cow, the giant and the little old woman.
● Encourage volunteers to take it in turns to hold a magic bean and present a phrase from the story in the character's magic voice. Can the other children guess which character it is?

Differentiation
For older/more confident learners: Encourage use of gesture and movement to create more of a performance.
For younger/less confident learners: Provide a sentence to which children can match a voice.

Who am I?

Objective: To listen to others in class, ask relevant questions and follow instructions.
What you need: Copies of *Jack and the Beanstalk*, a large sheet of paper and a pen.
Cross-curricular link: Drama.

What to do

● Ask the children to go through the book to remind themselves of all the characters or important objects in the story of *Jack and the Beanstalk*.
● Working together, list these on the large piece of paper
● Now, list the numbers 1 to 10 further down the piece of paper. Ask a volunteer to choose one of the characters from the list but tell them to keep who they have chosen a secret.
● Invite the rest of the class to ask questions one at a time to which the volunteer can only reply yes or no. Encourage the children to find

out important information by asking questions such as: Are they living/not living? Where might you find them? Do they make certain noises? Do they grow? Write down the children's questions on the piece of paper.
● Once the children have asked ten questions, invite them to guess the character, or object, or reveal the answer yourself.
● Repeat the activity for different characters or objects, choosing a different child each time to answer the ten questions posed by the rest of the class.

Differentiation
For older/more confident learners: Challenge the children to work without first compiling the list of characters and objects.
For younger/less confident learners: Allow less confident learners to choose a friend to help them answer the questions.

Plot, character and setting

Climb the beanstalk

> **Objective:** To explore familiar themes and characters through play.
> **What you need:** Photocopiable page 18, paper counters, some coins (four for each pair of children).
> **Cross-curricular link:** Maths.

What to do

● Arrange the children into pairs. Give each pair a shared copy of the game on photocopiable page 18, four coins and cut-out giant and Jack paper counters.

● Explain that the aim of the game is to take turns to toss a coin, move up the beanstalk and be the first to reach the top of the beanstalk.

● Tell the children to place three of their coins at the top of the beanstalk and use the fourth as the dice. Players take it in turns to throw the coin. If it lands on heads, the player moves their counter up one leaf. If it lands on tails, the player moves their counter down a leaf (or off the beanstalk if a tail is thrown from the bottom leaf).

● Explain to the children that they should also follow any instructions written on the leaves they land on.

● The first person to climb the beanstalk picks up a coin and starts again from the bottom. The first player to collect two coins is the winner.

> **Differentiation**
> **For older/more confident learners:** Ask children to create their own ideas for a Jack and the Beanstalk themed game.
> **For younger/less confident learners:** Provide support to help children play the game.

Hide and seek

> **Objective:** To tell real and imagined stories using the conventions of familiar story language.
> **What you need:** A set of doll's house furniture or boxes, a play figure to represent Jack.

What to do

● Read through the book together and discuss where Jack had to hide. Ask the children to suggest other places where Jack could have hidden, for example, in a can of giant beans, in a shoe.

● Ask the children to help you label and illustrate each box (or piece of furniture) to match their suggestions.

● Choose a child to close their eyes while another child places Jack inside one of the boxes/pieces of furniture. When ready, invite the class to tell the child to open their eyes. Explain that this child is now the giant. He or she stands up and in a giant-like voice says *Fee, fi, fo, fum! …I smell the blood of a stinky man!*

● The giant then guesses which box Jack is hiding in. They are allowed two goes.

● If needed, allow the class to provide a clue before the child's second attempt.

● Repeat the game to give others the chance of being the giant. Let the children play the game in smaller groups once they have got the hang of it.

> **Differentiation**
> **For older/more confident learners:** Challenge children to plan, make and decorate their own 3D model hiding places prior to playing the game.
> **For younger/less confident learners:** Play hide and seek, with one child (the seeker) acting the role of the giant.

Noisy giant

● Use the musical instruments to make the noises you might hear in the following pictures.

Fee, Fi, Fo, Fum! ...I smell the blood of a stinky man!

Illustrations © 2011, Paul Hutchinson.

Plot, character and setting

Swap

- Carefully draw four things that are important to you that are not already on the sheet.
- Cut out the cards and play 'Swap' with your partner.

Magic goose	Harp
Magic bean	Sack of gold

Illustrations © 2011, Paul Hutchinson.

READ & RESPOND: Activities based on Jack and the Beanstalk

Plot, character and setting

Scavenger hunt

● Find these objects in the story.

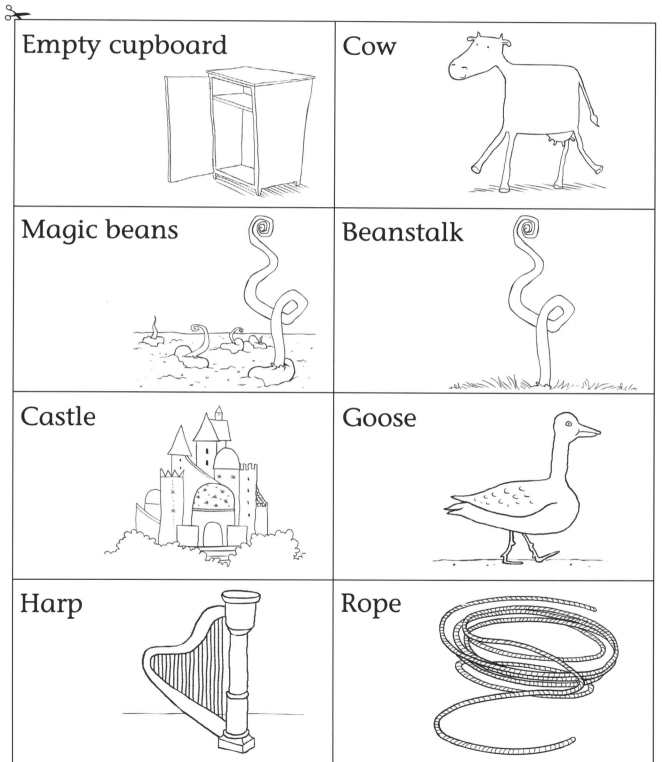

Empty cupboard	Cow
Magic beans	Beanstalk
Castle	Goose
Harp	Rope

Climb the beanstalk

- Place three of your coins at the top of the beanstalk. Use your fourth coin as your dice.
- If you throw heads, move up one leaf. If you throw tails, move down one leaf. Follow any other instructions on the leaf you land on.
- When you reach the top, take a coin and start the climb again. The first player to collect two coins is the winner.

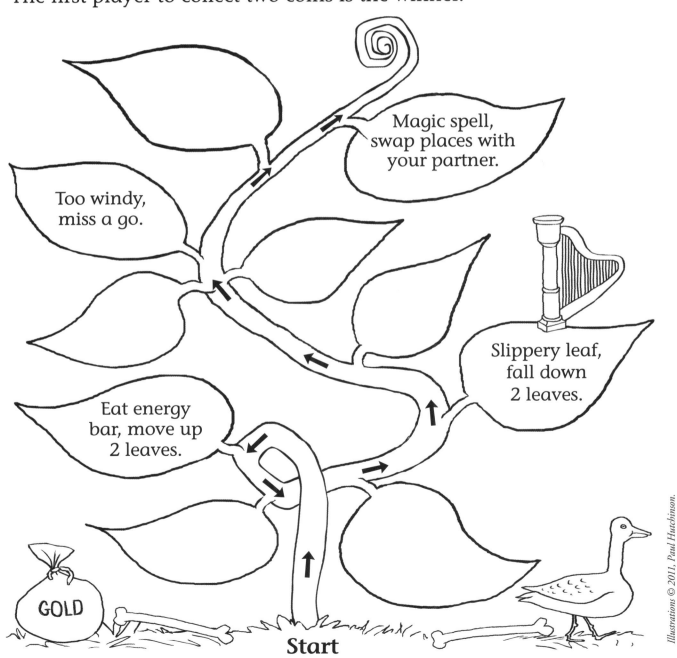

Too windy, miss a go.

Magic spell, swap places with your partner.

Slippery leaf, fall down 2 leaves.

Eat energy bar, move up 2 leaves.

GOLD

Start

Illustrations © 2011, Paul Hutchinson.

Talk about it

Dreaming

Objective: To listen to talk by an adult, remember some specific points and identify what they have learned.
What you need: Paper, cushions or soft blankets, soothing music, low-level lighting, joss sticks or fragrant oils.
Cross-curricular link: PSHE.

What to do

● Prepare the setting in advance to make it a warm, comfortable area. Explain to the children that they are going to relax and daydream. Turn on the music and ask the children to lie down and make themselves comfortable.
● Talk in a soothing voice and encourage the children to close their eyes. Invite them to allow their minds to daydream without talking. Ask the children to imagine that they are asleep in bed while a beanstalk grows outside. Think about how the beanstalk moves and creeps. Ask: *How does it feel to climb through the clouds?*
● Then ask the children to imagine that they are at the castle. What can they see in their imaginations? Ask: *How do you feel? What can you see, smell and hear?*
● After about five minutes, slowly ask the children to 'wake' themselves up.
● Bring the group into a circle and share the children's experiences. Ask: *How do we know the difference between a dream and a daydream?*

Differentiation
For older/more confident learners: Ask children to consider the following question: How do we know we are not all asleep in bed having the same dream?
For younger/less confident learners: Encourage children to draw the images they had in their head to help them talk about the experience.

Through the keyhole

Objective: To ensure that everyone contributes, allocate tasks, and consider alternatives and reach an agreement.
What you need: An enlarged photocopiable page 22, an A4 piece of card with a keyhole shape cut out of the middle (approximately 6–8cm), Blu-Tack®, a 'yes' and 'no' card.
Cross-curricular links: PSHE, history.

What to do

● Prepare in advance by placing the keyhole over one of the pictures on the photocopiable sheet and display both on the board. Explain to the class that they must guess from your clues who might be behind the door and then decide collectively whether that person should be allowed in.
● Display the 'yes' and 'no' cards on either side of the board. Say: 'Knock, knock' and invite the children to reply 'Who's there?' Provide clues until the children guess the correct answer.
● When they have worked it out, ask them to vote either 'Yes, they may come in' or 'No, they cannot' by moving to the 'yes' or 'no' side of the board.
● Ask the children to sit facing each other in their groups of 'yes' and 'no'. Encourage members of both groups to say why they made that decision and invite the other side to respond with counter arguments. Ask if anyone wishes to change their mind and, if so, why.
● Repeat the activity with the second picture.

Differentiation
For older/more confident learners: Encourage children to choose their own historical or fictional figure for the activity.
For younger/less confident learners: Help less confident talkers rehearse their ideas by allowing talk with a partner who has made the same choice.

Talk about it

Treasure snatch

Objective: To ask and answer questions, make relevant contributions, offer suggestions and take turns.
What you need: A set of eight laminated cards cut out from photocopiable page 23, a skipping rope or length of string.
Cross-curricular link: Philosophy.

What to do
● Ask the children what they think their most valuable possession is and why.
● Explain that Jack has only got a short time to escape down the beanstalk with his six treasures before the giant wakes up. He can only carry one object at a time. The children should help Jack choose from the cards which items he should take in which order and why.
● Spread the skipping rope along the floor like a beanstalk. Place the 'most important' card at the bottom and the 'least important' card at the top. Ask for a volunteer to choose a card and

place it at the appropriate place on the beanstalk. Repeat until all six objects are arranged along the beanstalk.
● Ask the children whether there are any items they think should be moved. Encourage them to discuss their reasons. Ask: *What does this item represent? Is that more or less important than…? Why?*
● Can the children agree a definite order of importance? Which objects caused the most problems?

Differentiation
For older/more confident learners: Challenge children to make their own beanstalks and draw pictures of their most treasured possessions in the order they would rescue them.
For younger/less confident learners: Ask children to think first about what their most valuable possession is and draw it on a beanstalk before completing this activity.

Story stick

Objective: To tell real and imagined stories using the conventions of familiar story language.
What you need: A copy of *Jack and the Beanstalk*, a stick or metre ruler, strips of material, ribbons, wool, feathers, beads.

What to do
● Explain to the children that they are going to become storytellers like the one who tells Jack's tale. Look through the book together and find interesting examples of the language he uses. (*I'm not going to start by saying… a little bit of this…*)
● Ask the children to work together to make a storyteller's tool called a story stick. The children should decorate the stick with ribbons, material, feathers, wool, beads or other adornments that might be available.
● When the stick is finished, ask the children to sit in a story circle. Start the story off with a

phrase such as 'I'm not going to say that Jack was lazy, but…'.
● Encourage the children to take it in turns to hold the stick and tell the next part of the story, then pass the stick on to the next child to hold.
● Continue to pass the stick around the circle until the children feel the story has ended. Allow children to 'pass' if they find this tricky, but encourage them to think of or join in with whole-class choruses or sound effects.

Differentiation
For older/more confident learners: Encourage children to make up their own versions of the story using devices such as cliffhangers,
For younger/less confident learners: Encourage less confident talkers to add sound effects to parts of the story. Provide support in small groups to practise telling the story first.

Talk about it

Beanstalk enquiry

> **Objective:** To ask and answer questions, make relevant contributions, offer suggestions and take turns.
> **What you need:** A copy of *Jack and the Beanstalk*, four large sheets of paper, pens.
> **Cross-curricular links:** PSHE, philosophy.

What to do

● Read *Jack and the Beanstalk*. Ask the children to think about the main events of the story. Write one of the following headings at the top of each piece of paper: Theft; Laziness; Wealth; Justice. Discuss what each concept means.

● Ask the children to think about which of the main events of the story might fit under which heading. Record their responses on the corresponding sheet.

● Place each sheet in a different corner of the room. Explain to the children that you would like them to choose one area of the story to think

about in more depth. They should then move to their chosen corner. Encourage them to talk in their groups about why they are interested in that part of the story.

● Ask each group to create one question relevant to their chosen concept, write it on the sheet and bring it back to the talking circle.

● Read out each question and ask the children to vote on which one they would like to enquire about together.

> **Differentiation**
> **For older/more confident learners:** Encourage children with experience of philosophy to decide which concepts are present in the story and ask a variety of questions related to these
> **For younger/less confident learners:** Provide support to enable children to turn statements into questions through the use of sensitive modelling.

Treasure hunt

> **Objective:** To listen to and follow instructions accurately, asking for help and clarification if necessary.
> **What you need:** An enlarged photocopiable page 24 as well as copies for each pair, pencils,
> **Cross-curricular links:** Geography, maths.

What to do

● Think about the treasures that the giant owned. Explain that the giant locks his treasure away at night to keep it safe. Challenge the children to help Jack follow the little old woman's instructions in the dark to find it.

● Show the enlarged map (photocopiable page 24). Explain to the children that Jack can only move up to three squares horizontally (east/west) or vertically (north/south) at a time.

● Draw an item of treasure in a square on the top row. Ask the children to give Jack a command, for example, 'Move three squares west'. Mark

his progress by putting a cross on each square he lands on.

● Continue until Jack reaches the item. Jack must be manoeuvred around any obstacles.

● Provide each child with a photocopiable sheet and ask them to work in pairs. They should face each other and draw some treasure in a secret location on their grid. They then should take it in turns to give a command which their partner marks off. If they land on a hazard the move does not count and they miss a turn.

● The first person to reach the treasure is the winner.

> **Differentiation**
> **For older/more confident learners:** Ask children to design their own grids with more hazards.
> **For younger/less confident learners:** Allow children to work in small groups, taking turns to give an instruction.

Through the keyhole

- Who is behind the door? Will you let them in?

Illustrations © 2011, Paul Hutchinson.

Treasure snatch

● Cut out these cards and order them from most to least important.

Most important	Least important

Illustrations © 2011, Paul Hutchinson.

READ & RESPOND: Activities based on Jack and the Beanstalk

Talk about it

SECTION 5

Treasure hunt

- Face your partner and draw your treasure in a secret location on your grid.
- Take it in turns with your partner to give a command such as 'Move three squares west'.
- Mark off the squares you land on.
- If you land on a hazard you must miss a turn.
- The first player to reach the treasure is the winner!

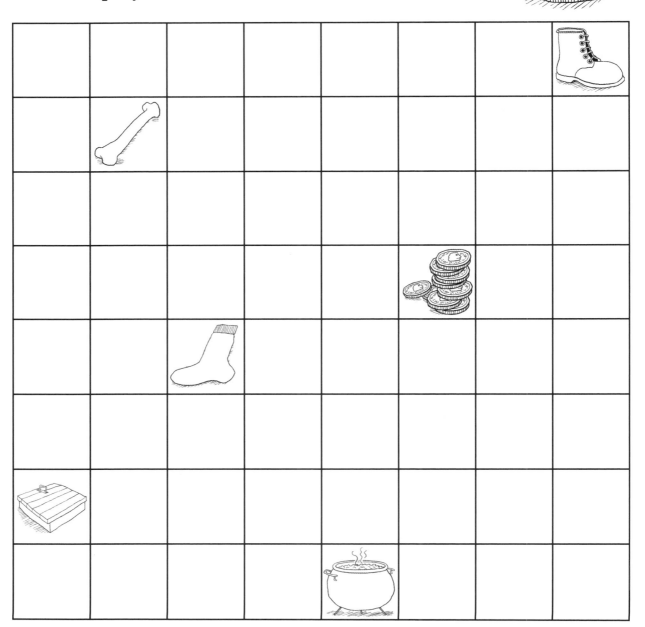

Illustrations © 2011, Paul Hutchinson.

Get writing

Cow for sale

> **Objective:** To draw on knowledge and experience
> of texts in deciding and planning what and how
> to write.
> **What you need:** Copies of *Jack and the Beanstalk*,
> photocopiable page 28, drawing equipment.
> **Cross-curricular link:** Science.

What to do

● Look together at the book, paying particular
attention to the drawing of Daisy the cow. Explain
that Jack is feeling so lazy today that he can't take
Daisy to market. Ask the children to think of
all the different ways Jack could let people know
that he has a cow for sale. (Newspaper adverts,
internet, shop window cards, leaflets or flyers,
TV advert, and so on.)
● Explain that Jack would like the children's help
in creating some posters that they could put up
around the village advertising that Daisy is for
sale. Write the following headings on the board
or a large piece of paper: Name of cow; Reason
for sale; Why people should want the cow; What
you would be willing to swap for the cow. Ask
the children to think and talk together about
these headings and share their ideas.
● Give photocopiable page 28 to each child and
ask them to write and illustrate their posters.
Ensure that the children write something to
cover each heading.

> **Differentiation**
> **For older/more confident learners:** Challenge
> children to write additional adverts in different
> formats, looking first at examples of different written
> advertisements from newspapers and the internet.
> **For younger/less confident learners:** Provide
> children with a bank of words from their ideas.

Magic beans instructions

> **Objective:** To convey information and ideas in
> simple non-narrative forms.
> **What you need:** Copies of *Jack and the Beanstalk*,
> surgical gloves, soil, a selection of beans and pictures
> of what they look like when grown, such as runner
> beans, baked beans, broad beans, aduki beans,
> jumping beans, jelly beans and some beans painted a
> strange colour.
> **Cross-curricular link:** Science.

What to do

● Look back through the book together and
ask the children if they can remember what
the funny little man said about the beans. (He
mentioned that he had lost their instructions.)
● Begin by asking the children to think of as
many sorts of beans as they can. Show them
some beans and ask if they can identify them and
match them to the pictures. Ask: *Which beans
will grow and which might not?*

● Explore with the children when beans might
not grow. Ask: *What do beans need to grow?* (Soil,
light, water.)
● Hang some surgical gloves near a window
using strong pins or staples. Help the children
to fill a finger each with soil and plant one of the
beans in it.
● Now ask the children to write instructions
for planting the beans. They should include: the
date it was planted; the type of bean used; how
to plant it; conditions for growth; information
about what it will grow into.

> **Differentiation**
> **For older/more confident learners:** Challenge
> children to write a diary recording their
> bean's growth.
> **For younger/less confident learners:** Provide a bank
> of useful words from the children's ideas.

Get writing

Power beans

> **Objective:** To draw together ideas and information from across a whole text, using simple signposts in the text.
> **What you need:** A copy of *Jack and the Beanstalk*, a handful of painted beans.
> **Cross-curricular link:** Drama.

What to do

● Focus on the spread where the beans are starting to grow. How does the illustrator capture the idea that these beans are magical? Ask: *What happened when these beans were planted?*

● Ask the children to imagine that all beans have different powers and their beanstalks lead you to many different lands. Show the children your beans. Do they look magic?

● Explain to the children that they are going to write some pages for a magic beanstalk guide book. Ask them to close their eyes and imagine what sort of magic lands there might be at the top of a beanstalk. Everyone might be as tall as giants; they might be able to fly; or the land might be ruled by evil kittens. Encourage lots of ideas, the stranger the better.

● Now ask the children to write a description of their imaginary place. Make sure they include details of what sort of land it is, who they see and what strange things happen. Is it a good place to visit or not?

> **Differentiation**
> **For older/more confident learners:** Give children travel brochures to look at and ask them to emulate the style of writing that would entice people to visit.
> **For younger/ less confident learners:** Use drama and role play to rehearse and build confidence. Support children in their own writing.

Gruesome giant food

> **Objective:** To draw on knowledge and experience of texts in deciding and planning what and how to write.
> **What you need:** Recipe books, photocopiable page 29 (one enlarged and one for each child), drawing equipment.
> **Cross-curricular link:** Food technology.

What to do

● Look together at the enlarged photocopiable page 29. Ask: *What do you see? Who do you think the cooking pot might belong to? Why?*

● Explain that the giant is always hungry and the little old woman is running out of recipes that he likes. Allow the class some time to look through the recipe books and find things that they might like to eat and that the giant may like too.

● Look together at the format of a page in a recipe book. Notice that the ingredients are listed first and then the method describes how to make the dish (in a numbered step-by-step format which makes it easy to follow).

● Ask the children to think about food that the giant might like. Try to encourage them to use their imaginations and think of things that humans would not like to eat. Record their ideas.

● Talk together about ways to cook these ingredients and what they will look like when cooked.

● Now ask the children to write up their gruesome giant recipes on their recipe pages.

> **Differentiation**
> **For older/more confident learners:** Encourage children to devise and write a menu for a three-course giant banquet.
> **For younger/less confident learners:** Encourage children to use a word bank and illustrate their recipe using labels instead of whole sentences.

Get writing

I'm rich (shopping list)

> **Objective:** To convey information and ideas in simple non-narrative forms.
> **What you need:** Copies of *Jack and the Beanstalk*, a bag of gold coins.
> **Cross-curricular link:** Maths.

What to do

● Look through the book together and find the page where we see the giant's sacks of gold. Ask the children to consider how much money each sack might contain.

● Challenge them to count how many sacks there are. Ask: *Can you work out exactly how many gold coins there are if each bag has 100 coins in it?* Tell them that, in fact, there is one million pounds' worth of gold altogether.

● Explore with the children how this money will help Jack. Ask: *What will he be able to do with it? Will it change his life? In what ways?*

● Encourage the children to talk together about what they would do with one million pounds. Would they use it to help others, for example, through donations to charities? Which charities would they choose? Why? Ask: *What would you buy for yourself? Would you share it with others or keep it for yourself?*

● After this talking and thinking time ask the children to create a shopping list of what they would do or buy with one million pounds.

> **Differentiation**
> **For older/more confident learners:** Ask children to write an explanation of why they chose to spend their money in the ways they chose.
> **For younger/less confident learners:** Allow children to illustrate their lists and support their writing if needed.

Postcard to Mum

> **Objective:** To sustain form in narrative, including use of person and time.
> **What you need:** Copies of *Jack and the Beanstalk*, photocopiable page 30, examples of postcards to look at.
> **Cross-curricular link:** Geography.

What to do

● Look together at the selection of postcards. Talk about why people send postcards. Ask: *What sorts of pictures do they have on them? Why?*

● Look at some examples of writing on them. Where does the address go? Look at how much space there is available to write in. How does the message on a postcard differ from the message in a letter or a text message on a phone?

● Look through the book and ask the children to watch for any illustrations that suggest where Jack is so he can write a postcard to his mum.

● Give each child their own postcard (photocopiable page 30) and tell them that they need to cut out the postcard template first. Ask the children to draw what the land of the giant looks like on one side and write a message from Jack to his mother on the other, explaining that they are writing as Jack.

● Remind the children to create an address to send it to, making sure they write it on the correct side of their postcard.

> **Differentiation**
> **For older/more confident learners:** Challenge children to write a longer letter from Jack to his mum.
> **For younger/less confident learners:** Support children in their writing using sound or keyword banks.

Cow for sale

- Make Daisy the cow look beautiful so that someone will want to buy her.
- Write a title at the top of the page.
- Add a description and reason for sale at the bottom of the page.

Title _____

_____

_____

_____

_____

Illustrations © 2011, Paul Hutchinson.

READ & RESPOND: Activities based on Jack and the Beanstalk

Get writing

Gruesome giant food

● Can you invent a delicious recipe for the giant to eat?

Ingredients

_____

_____

_____

_____

_____

_____

_____

Method

1. _____

_____

2. _____

_____

3. _____

_____

4. _____

_____

Illustrations © 2011, Paul Hutchinson.

Postcard to Mum

- Cut out the postcard.
- Draw a picture of the giant's land on the blank side of the postcard.
- Write Jack's message on the other side. Remember to write the address on the right!

SCHOLASTIC

Assessment

Assessment advice

Richard Walker and Niamh Sharkey's version of this classic and well-loved tale will emphasise the importance of storytelling as an art form. Stories such as these have traditionally been passed down from generation to generation. It is vitally important in today's technological age that we do not allow our children to lose sight of this valuable tradition of oral storytelling. The following assessment will serve as a visual aid in their quest as storytellers.

Jack and the Beanstalk provides many opportunities to talk about, think about and play with the genre of traditional tales. It offers opportunities to assess the language of story, the understanding of clear-cut beginning, middle and end structures and the passage of time in a sequenced manner. It also provides plentiful opportunities for children to explore the playfulness of the spoken word, allowing them to immerse themselves in role play, drama, song and dance activities. The children will enjoy experimenting with repetition, and familiar phrases, such as *Fee, Fi, Fo, Fum* which provokes a powerful image and is guaranteed to stay in the memory for a lifetime.

The learning opportunities allow for scientific and geographical research and understanding. The story presents opportunities to explore the environment and create new worlds. It also requires children to be inventive and to think imaginatively, developing artistic and creative skills. The nature of the book allows children to engage in a text that brings characters to life through performance skills, which leads to better understanding of character, setting and plot and stimulates discussion about all these elements.

Beanstalk storyboard

> **Assessment focus:** To assess understanding of the sequence of events in a story; to retell stories in their own words.
> **What you need:** Photocopiable page 32 for each child.

What to do

● Give out photocopiable page 32 and look at it together. What do the children see? (They see a beanstalk which has eight leaves on it.) Each empty leaf represents a part of the story from *Jack and the Beanstalk*.

● Ask the children to reflect quietly on what the major parts of the story were. Explain that there are not enough leaves on the beanstalk to record everything that happens in the book, so they have to think carefully about the eight most important and memorable moments in the book. The lowest leaf on the beanstalk represents the first important event and the following events should be recorded on the leaves rising up the beanstalk.

● Ask the children to record the story information pictorially.

● When the beanstalks are finished, bring the children together and ask them to share their beanstalk stories. They should embellish their storyboards to give as accurate a portrayal of the story as they can.

● Do all of the children use the same eight points? What was the first event that was common to most storyboards and which was the last?

● Ask the children to choose one illustration from their beanstalk that would make a good front cover of a book. Can they explain why?

Beanstalk storyboard

● Draw a picture on each leaf showing the most important or most memorable parts of the story.

Start at the bottom of the beanstalk

READ & RESPOND: Activities based on Jack and the Beanstalk